Collins

easy learning

Problem solving and reasoning workbook

Ages 7–9

£2.00 per kg

Tom Hall

How to use this book

- Easy Learning workbooks help your child improve basic skills, build confidence and develop a love of learning.

- Find a quiet, comfortable place to work, away from distractions.

- Get into a routine of completing one or two workbook pages with your child every day.

- Ask your child to circle the star that matches how many questions they have completed every two pages:

Some = half of the questions   Most = more than half   All = all the questions

- Encourage your child to work through all of the questions eventually, and praise them for completing them.

- This book contains lots of problem-solving and reasoning activities for your child to complete. Your child will have to select and apply the appropriate number, measurement and/or geometry skills to solve each problem.

- Encourage your child to break down the activities in order to work them out, and to make notes and drawings to help them.

- If your child is struggling with an activity, discuss with them what they know, what they need to find out and how they might go about it.

- Accessibility of content will be dependent on what your child has already covered in school and, at the lower age range in particular, your child may find some activities unfamiliar and/or very challenging. If so, leave them and move on, then revisit them at a later date.

Parent tip
Look out for tips on how to help your child.

Published by Collins
An imprint of HarperCollins*Publishers*
1 London Bridge Street
London SE1 9GF

© HarperCollins*Publishers* 2020

10 9 8 7 6 5 4 3 2 1

ISBN 978-0-00-838791-4

The author asserts the moral right to be identified as the author of this work.

British Library Cataloguing in Publication Data

A catalogue record for this publication is available from the British Library

Author: Tom Hall
Commissioning editor: Fiona McGlade
Text design and layout: Jouve India Private Limited
Illustrations: © HarperCollins*Publishers* and © Shutterstock.com
Cover design: Sarah Duxbury
Project editor: Katie Galloway
Production: Karen Nulty
Printed in Great Britain by Martins the Printers

Contents

How to use this book   2

At the zoo   4

Secret numbers   6

At the market   8

Sports day   10

At the rugby match   12

Cake and pizza   14

At the fruit and vegetable stall   16

Pocket money   18

A day at school   20

At the park   22

Shapes   24

Back at the zoo   26

After-school club   28

School dinners   29

On the train   30

Answers   31

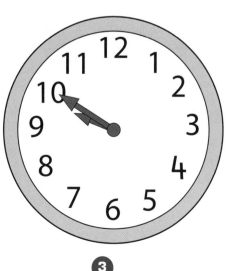

At the zoo

1 Some antelope arrive at the zoo in a large lorry. The lorry is divided into sections that hold 4 antelope.
As the antelope are unloaded, Ben counts them in fours: 4, 8, 12, 16, 20 …
What are the next **five** numbers Ben says to count all the antelope?

24	28	32	36	40

Sally checks Ben's count, but she counts in eights.
What numbers does Sally say to count all the antelope?

8	16	24	32	40

Ben and Sally count the sacks of antelope feed. There are fewer than 50 sacks.
Ben says, 'If I count the sacks in sixes, I can put six sacks on each shelf and there are none left over.'
Sally says, 'Count them in sevens. Put seven on each shelf and there will be none left over.'
How many sacks of feed are there? | 0 |

Parent tip
For Question 2, discuss the meaning of the zeros at the beginning of the digital counter.

2 At the zoo's entrance, a machine counts visitors in fifties.
Through the day the machine reads:

0	0	0	0		0	0	5	0		0	1	0	0		0	1	5	0		0	2	0	0

What will the next five displays show?

0	2	5	0		0	3	0	0		0	3	5	0		0	4	0	0		0	4	5	0

3 The total number of visitors to the zoo each day for a week is recorded.

Sunday	Monday	Tuesday	Wednesday	Thursday	Friday	Saturday
731	690	821	622	832	821	812

Put <, > or = in the circles to compare the number of visitors each day.

Monday (<) Tuesday   Wednesday (<) Sunday

Tuesday (=) Friday   Thursday (>) Saturday

4 The total number of visitors to the zoo each month for the first 6 months of the year is recorded.

January	February	March	April	May	June
1,854	2,476	5,921	5,096	5,934	5,261

Put **<**, **>** or **=** in the circles to compare the number of visitors each month.

January February

May April

June April

May March

Parent tip
Discuss the importance of place value when comparing numbers.

5 The visitors to the zoo vote for their favourite animal.
The top five most popular animals are:

Animal	Chimps	Elephants	Giraffes	Lions	Tigers
Number of votes	2,068	1,278	2,416	2,463	2,506

Write the animals in order, most popular first.

chimp	grass	lion	tiger	graf

elaf and chimps

Most popular   Least popular

6 The zoo is trying to attract more visitors.
If monthly numbers increase by 1,000, what would the new monthly totals be?

Increase	January	February	March	April	May	June
160000	1,854	2,476	5,921	5,096	5,934	5,261
+1,000						

How did you do?

Questions 1–6

Circle the star to show how you have done.

 Some

Most

 All

Secret numbers

1 Sam writes some numbers and then describes them.

Draw lines to match the numbers with the descriptions.

| 23 |
| 74 |
| 49 |
| 92 |
| 37 |

is a number with four tens.

is a number with two ones.

is three ones less than 40.

is a number with two tens.

is three tens more than 40.

Parent tip
Remember that a number has the value of the column it is placed in, e.g. 2 in the tens column does not have a value of 2; the value is two tens or 20

2 Maisie uses place value cards to describe her secret number. Here are her place value cards.

| 1 ten | 8 ones | 7 tens | 9 ones | 4 tens | 5 ones |

How can Maisie use the cards to make:

the **smallest** 2-digit number?   ten 5

the **largest** 2-digit number?   7 tens nine one

the number **closest to 50**?   40

3 Ben says, '39 is larger than 41 because it has a 9 and 9 is a large number.'

Explain why Ben is **incorrect**.

becase its the tens that maters

4 What is the value of the numbers shown on these number lines?

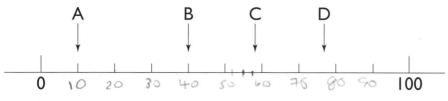

A = 10   B = 40   C = 56   D = 76

5 Samir has a secret number.
He says, 'My number has 9 ones and 3 tens.'

What is Samir's secret number? 39

Mandy also has a secret number.
She says, 'My number has two tens more than Samir's number and two fewer ones.'
What is Mandy's secret number? 57

Parent tip
Talk through a problem, asking your child to use the facts that they are given to work out what answers might be.

6 What are the numbers shown on these abacuses?

Parent tip
Encourage your child to draw things to help them work out a problem.

A
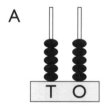

B

C

55   48   25

Ben uses **all** the beads on Abacus A to make a different number.
Write three different numbers that Ben could make.

46   37   19

Max takes **three** beads off Abacus C to make a different number.
Write three different numbers that Max could make.

22   13   4

How did you do?   **Questions 1–6**

Circle the star
to show how
you have done.

☆ Some   ★ Most   ★ All

7

At the market

1 David runs a clothes stall at the market. He sells T-shirts and keeps a record of the number he has for sale.
He orders 100 more T-shirts of each size.
How many will he have of each size?

Size	S	M	L	XL
Number	236	197	315	106
+ 100	326	297	415	206

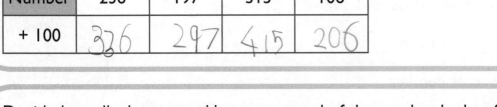

2 David also sells dresses and keeps a record of the number he has for sale.
He sells 10 dresses of each size to a local shop.
How many dresses of each size will he have left?

Size	10	12	14	16	18	20
Number	215	156	207	124	138	108
− 10	315	256	307	124	138	2408

3 This table shows the number of jumpers David has for sale.
Work out how many he has in total.

Size	S	M	L	XL	Total
Number	110	109	131	150	

During a week, David sells 94 jumpers.

How many jumpers will he have left? 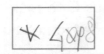 ✗ 4008

4 At the beginning of the week, David has 213 jackets for sale.
He buys 40 more jackets to sell.
By the end of the week, David has 142 jackets left for sale.

How many jackets did David sell? | 1 1 1 |

253
−142
‾‾‾‾
1 1 1

5 David works out how many pairs of socks he has for sale.
He has **333** pairs of men's socks and **269** pairs of women's socks.

How many pairs of socks does David have for sale altogether? 333
26P

602

Parent tip
Remember that to write the inverse of a calculation, your child must start with the answer.

David wants to check his calculation. Write an inverse calculation that David could use to check his calculation.

602 = 333 + 269

6 Every Saturday, David works out the total number of items sold that week. Then he adds up the total number of items sold in the first six months of the year. (Some months have five Saturdays.) Calculate each monthly total.

Jan	
Week 1	1 0 0 8
Week 2	1 1 2 6
Week 3	1 3 0 2
Week 4	+ 1 3 2 4
Total	4 7 6 0

Feb	
Week 1	9 3 4
Week 2	1 0 0 7
Week 3	9 2 7
Week 4	+ 1 0 3 2
Total	3 9 0 0

Mar	
Week 1	8 9 1
Week 2	9 2 2
Week 3	1 0 8 4
Week 4	1 0 3 2
Week 5	+ 1 2 0 9
Total	5 7 4 0

These calculations have a missing number. Find the missing number.

Apr	
Week 1	1 0 0 6
Week 2	1 2 0 2
Week 3	1 0 0 8
Week 4	+ 1 0 1 5
Total	4 2 3 1

May	
Week 1	9 0 5
Week 2	1 1 2 0
Week 3	1 0 6 2
Week 4	9 2 4
Week 5	+ 1 3 8 0
Total	4 9 9 1

Jun	
Week 1	9 2 4
Week 2	8 1 7
Week 3	9 9 4
Week 4	+ 1 5
Total	3 7 4 0

Sports day

1 Children are put into teams for sports day.
In Year 3, there are 48 children. How many children will there be in each team, if there are:

3 teams? `H44`   4 teams? `1ρ2`   6 teams? `288`

In Year 4, there are 36 children. How many children will there be in each team, if there are:

3 teams? `108`   4 teams? `1844`   6 teams? `216`

In Year 5, there are 60 children. How many children will there be in each team, if there are:

3 teams? `180`   4 teams? `210`   6 teams? `2010`

In Year 6, there are 56 children. The teachers need to decide whether the Year 6 children will be divided into 3, 4 or 6 teams. There must be an equal number of children in each team.
What do you think the teachers will decide? Explain your choice.

_____

_____

Parent tip Learning multiplication and division facts by heart will help your child to work quickly.

2 In the novelty race, different objects are laid out in each lane.
There are 8 hoops, 4 bean bags and 2 skipping ropes.

If there are 8 lanes, each with the same equipment, how many hoops, bean bags and skipping ropes are there?

`64` hoops   `32` bean bags   `16` ropes

In the potato race, an **equal** number of potatoes is set out in each of the 8 lanes for children to collect, one at a time. The teachers have a sack of 70 potatoes.

What is the greatest number of potatoes that can be laid in each lane? `8`

3 In another race, teams of children must race with 8 tennis balls, 5 footballs and 4 rugby balls each.

How many of each type of ball will be needed for 6 teams?

 tennis balls   footballs   rugby balls

In the long-distance running race, 4 teams of 6 children take part.

The track is 245 metres long and the children must run around the track 5 times.

How many children take part in the race?

How long is the long-distance race?   1223 / 1225

```
  245
    5
-----
 1225
```

4 Points are awarded for each race. In an individual race, first place is awarded 6 points; second place is awarded 4 points; and third place is awarded 3 points. Team races are awarded double points. The tables show the results for the Blue Team.

> **Parent tip**
> Remember to use a written method to calculate harder multiplications. Your child does not have to work out everything mentally.

Fill in the tables to show the total number of points awarded.

Individual races			
1st place (6 points)	12 places	=	72
2nd place (4 points)	8 places	=	32
3rd place (3 points)	6 places	=	18
Total for individual races			

Team races			
1st place (12 points)	6 places	=	
2nd place (8 points)	3 places	=	24
3rd place (6 points)	2 places	=	8
Total for team races			

What was the total number of points awarded to the Blue Team?

At the rugby match

1 This is the plan of a rugby ground.

North Stand
2,750 seats and 2,200 standing

West Stand
1,975 seats and
2,390 standing

Rugby pitch

East Stand
2,435 seats and
1,645 standing

South Stand
2,500 seats and 2,450 standing

```
  2435
+ 1,645
  4080
```

How many fans can there be in total in the:

North Stand? [4,950]   East Stand? [4080]

```
  1975
+ 2,390
  4365
```

South Stand? [4950]   West Stand? [4365]

How many fans will the ground hold altogether? [18345]

2 Some of the visiting fans arrive in coaches. Each coach is full.

- 9 coaches have 55 seats.
- 7 coaches have 45 seats.

How many visiting fans arrive by coach? [100]

Other fans arrive by car.

- 129 cars each carry 4 fans.
- 146 cars each carry 3 fans.
- 178 cars each carry 2 fans.

How many visiting fans arrive by car? [   ]

All the visiting fans go into the West Stand.

How many empty spaces are left in the West Stand? [   ]

3 The home fans are in the North, East and South Stands.

Calculate how many tickets are left for sale in these stands.
(Use the seat numbers from Question 1.)

North Stand: 3,256 tickets sold

East Stand: 2,764 tickets sold

South Stand: 3,863 tickets sold

Parent tip
Remind your child to always read the question very carefully and make sure they know what it is they need to work out.

4 The rugby club puts 840 programmes for sale in each of the four stands.

Then, they share the programmes between the number of entrances to each stand. All the programmes are sold.

At the North Stand there are eight entrances.
How many programmes are there at each entrance?

At the East Stand there are six entrances.
How many programmes are there at each entrance?

At the South Stand there are seven entrances.
How many programmes are there at each entrance?

At the West Stand there are five entrances.
How many programmes are there at each entrance?

The club prints 3,750 programmes altogether.
How many programmes are left over?

135 of the leftover programmes are put aside.
The rest are sent to the club shop.
How many programmes are sent to the club shop?

How did you do?   **Questions 1–4**

Circle the star to show how you have done.

 Some

Most

 All

Cake and pizza

1 Sophie's birthday cake is decorated with 30 strawberries and 20 raspberries.
The cake is cut into 10 pieces. 9 pieces are eaten.
The strawberries and raspberries are equally divided between the slices.

What fraction of the cake is eaten? ☐   How many strawberries are on each slice? ☐

What fraction of the cake is left? ☐   How many raspberries are on each slice? ☐

2 In a cake shop window, there are 12 cakes on display.

Coffee cake   Chocolate cake   Sponge cake

Fruit cake   Carrot cake

What fraction of the cakes are:

carrot cakes? ☐   chocolate cakes? ☐

Ned says, 'Half of the cakes are fruit cakes and carrot cakes.'
Explain why Ned is correct.

Parent tip
Explain that some fractions are the same. Work on further examples of equivalent fractions.

3 A school buys 10 pizzas for an end-of-term party. Each pizza is cut into 10 pieces.

What fraction is one piece of all 10 pizzas? ☐

The school also buys a large rectangular cake for the end-of-term party.

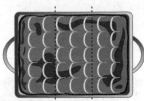

The teacher cuts the cake into thirds.
Complete the set of equivalent fractions for thirds.

Parent tip
Make sure your child understands the meaning of the numerator and denominator. In Question 3, make sure they realise what the denominator is.

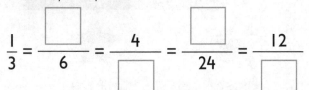

$$\frac{1}{3} = \frac{\Box}{6} = \frac{4}{\Box} = \frac{\Box}{24} = \frac{12}{\Box}$$

14

4 Mizzi visits a coffee shop. Some cakes have been cut into slices.
The number of slices depends on the size of the cake.
Some slices have been sold. The shaded pieces of cake are still for sale.

Lemon cake   Walnut cake   Berry cake   Banoffee pie

What fraction of each cake has been sold? What fraction of each cake is still for sale?

Lemon cake [ ] sold [ ] for sale

Walnut cake [ ] sold [ ] for sale

Berry cake [ ] sold [ ] for sale

Banoffee pie [ ] sold [ ] for sale

5 Dev, Ben, Obe and Josh all have similar pizzas cut into twelfths.

Dev eats $\frac{5}{12}$, Ben eats $\frac{8}{12}$, Obe eats $\frac{6}{12}$ and Josh eats $\frac{7}{12}$.

Write the boys' names in order, starting with the boy who ate the most.

[ ]   [ ]   [ ]   [ ]

ate the most   ate the least

How did you do?   **Questions 1–5**

Circle the star to show how you have done.

 Some   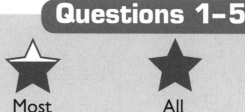 Most   All

At the fruit and vegetable stall

1 Jen buys some fruit. The fruit and the mass bought is shown below.
Write the fruit in order, starting with the heaviest.

bananas 2.15 kg	pears 2.34 kg	apples 1.07 kg	strawberries 1.91 kg	plums 2.09 kg

heaviest   lightest

2 George sells potatoes. Round these amounts of potatoes to the nearest whole kilogram.

2.3 kg [   ] kg   3.6 kg [   ] kg   5.8 kg [   ] kg   5.4 kg [   ] kg

If George sells the potatoes for 75p per kilogram, how much will he charge for each of the rounded masses of potatoes?

2.3 kg [£   ]   3.6 kg [£   ]   5.8 kg [£   ]   5.4 kg [£   ]

The customer who bought 3.6 kg of potatoes complained to George about his method of charging. Explain why you think the customer complained.

_____

_____

_____

3 George weighs the following vegetables.
What mass would they show if they were weighed on digital weighing scales showing kilograms?

$\frac{3}{4}$ kg of potatoes [   ] $\frac{1}{4}$ kg of parsnips [   ]

$\frac{1}{2}$ kg of onions [   ] $\frac{9}{10}$ kg of sprouts [   ]

$\frac{3}{10}$ kg of carrots [   ]

4 Harpreet pays for her shopping with a £20 note. Her shopping comes to £12.42

She uses £3.35 of her change to pay for her bus fare.

How much money does she have left? £ [ ]

5 George gets a delivery of 3 kilograms of garlic and 5 kilograms of mushrooms.

He divides the garlic equally into 10 bags.
What mass of garlic is in each bag? [ ] kg = [ ] g

George divides the mushrooms into 10 bags.
What mass of mushrooms is in each bag? [ ] kg = [ ] g

6 Kenny puts 5 pieces of each fruit into bags. George weighs the bags.
Kenny decides he is getting too much and asks George to take one piece out of each bag.
George re-weighs the bags with 4 pieces of fruit.
Find the mass of each piece of fruit George has taken out.

Fruit	Mass of 5 pieces	Mass of 4 pieces	Mass of 1 piece
apples	0.75 kg	0.56 kg	kg
pears	0.87 kg	0.64 kg	kg
oranges	1.43 kg	1.09 kg	kg
grapefruit	2.06 kg	1.43 kg	kg
melon	4.86 kg	3.68 kg	kg

7 Ari buys these items. Find the cost of each item.

1.25 kg of potatoes at £0.80 per kilogram. £ [ ]

2.5 kg of wholemeal flour at £1.20 per kilogram. £ [ ]

1.75 kg of beans at £1 per kilogram. £ [ ]

Parent tip
When attempting Question 7, your child could change the decimal to a known fraction and then use the fraction to find the cost.

How did you do?

Questions 1–7

Circle the star to show how you have done.

 Some

 Most

 All

Pocket money

1 Henry has some money in his money box.

Number the coins and notes **1–6** to put them in order, starting with the smallest amount.

2 Debbie has this money:

She buys these four items:

10p   £1.75   £3   70p

How much money does Debbie have left? £ ☐

3 What is the total of each of these sets of notes and coins?

            £ ☐

            £ ☐

             £ ☐

            £ ☐

4 Daisy wants to buy a book for 90p
She has three 20p coins and one 10p coin.
She needs some more money to buy the book.
She can do this in different ways.

Parent tip
Drawing a picture can help your child to visualise a problem. Drawing the coins may help with these questions.

How can she do this using:

one coin? _____   two coins? _____

three coins? _____   four coins? _____

---

5 Gemma has two 50p coins, three 20p coins, three 10p coins and three 5p coins.
She wants to buy an apple for 65p and a banana for 75p.

How much money will she have left? ☐

Dev wants to buy a pen for 83p.
The greatest number of coins that could be used to make 83p is eighty-three 1p coins.

What is the fewest number of coins that could be used to make 83p? ☐

How could you make 83p using six coins?

_____

---

6 Bob is arranging a trip to a museum. An adult ticket costs £12 and a child ticket costs £8

Bob spends £44 on tickets.

If Bob buys 1 adult ticket, how many child tickets does Bob buy? ☐

How did you do?   **Questions 1–6**

Circle the star to show how you have done.

 Some   Most   All

A day at school

1 These are the times of activities for Ben's class for one day at school.

Which lesson **starts** at quarter to twelve? _____

Which lesson **ends** at ten past two? _____

What is Ben doing at ten to two? _____

What is Ben doing at twenty-five to eleven? _____

How long did Ben spend reading? _____

Which lesson lasted exactly one hour? _____

8:50 a.m.	Start of school
9:05 a.m.	Maths
10:00 a.m.	Assembly
10:30 a.m.	Morning break
10:45 a.m.	English
11:45 a.m.	Reading
12:15 p.m.	Lunch time
1:20 p.m.	PE
2:10 p.m.	Art
3:15 p.m.	End of school
3:30 p.m.	Gym club
4:35 p.m.	End of gym club

2 These clocks show various times through Ben's school day.
Use the timetable in Question 1 to say what he is doing at these times.

_____   _____   _____

What time does lunch time end? Write your answer in **words**.

_____

3 Ben has five lessons today. Use the timetable in Question 1 to write the lessons in order of length, starting with the shortest.

Maths   English   Reading   PE   Art

shortest   longest

4 Use the timetable in Question 1 to help you answer these questions.

How many minutes is it until morning break?

[ ]

How many minutes is it since the English lesson started?

[ ]

How long is it from the end of lunch time to the end of school?

_____

5 Use the timetable in Question 1 to help you answer these questions.

Ben has a digital watch that shows 24-hour time.
Circle the time showing on Ben's watch at the start of school.

07:50　　**08:50**　　**09:50**　　**20:50**　　**21:50**

Circle the time showing on Ben's watch at the start of Art.

13:15　　**14:10**　　**15:35**　　**16:20**　　**17:10**

Circle the time showing on Ben's watch at the end of school.

13:30　　**14:30**　　**15:15**　　**16:30**　　**17:15**

Ben goes to Gym Club. It takes him 35 minutes to get home afterwards.

What time is showing on Ben's watch when he gets home?

[ ]

Parent tip
Remember when writing 12-hour digital time, use a.m. or p.m.
Remember when writing 24-hour digital time, use 4 digits.

6 The autumn term at Ben's school lasts 14 weeks. One of the weeks is a holiday and Ben isn't at school on Saturdays or Sundays.

How many days is Ben at school in the autumn term?

[ ]

How did you do?

Questions 1–6

Circle the star to show how you have done.

 Some

 Most

 All

At the park

1 This is the plan for three flower beds in the park. Each square on the plan is 1 m long and 1 m wide in real life.

What is the perimeter of each flower bed?

	1				2													

Flower bed 1 [   ] m

Flower bed 2 [   ] m

Flower bed 3 [   ] m

2 There is a play area in the park. It is divided into two different areas for different age groups. Each square on the plan is 1 m long and 1 m wide in real life.

What is the perimeter and area of each play area?

Play area 1

Play area 2

Play area 1   Perimeter: [   ] m   Area: [   ] m²

Play area 2   Perimeter: [   ] m   Area: [   ] m²

3 This is the plan of the park café building. Each square on the plan is 1 m long and 1 m wide in real life. Find the perimeter and the area of each section of the café building.

Café	Perimeter:	[ ] m	Area:	[ ] m²	
Toilets	Perimeter:	[ ] m	Area:	[ ] m²	
Kitchen	Perimeter:	[ ] m	Area:	[ ] m²	

4 There are other buildings in the park.
Find the perimeter and area of each of these buildings.

Office: The office is 10 metres long and 10 metres wide.

Perimeter: [ ] m   Area: [ ] m²

Greenhouse: The greenhouse is 40 metres long and 10 metres wide.

Perimeter: [ ] m   Area: [ ] m²

Stores: The stores are 15 metres long and 8 metres wide.

Perimeter: [ ] m   Area: [ ] m²

How did you do?   Questions 1–4

Circle the star to show how you have done.

☆ Some   ★ Most   ★ All

23

Shapes

1 Evie uses rectangles of different sizes to make letters.

L H V F T N

Which letters have rectangles that are perpendicular; that are parallel; that are both perpendicular and parallel; or that are neither perpendicular nor parallel?
Tick (✓) the boxes to complete the table.

Letter	L	H	V	F	T	N
Perpendicular rectangles						
Parallel rectangles						

2 Here are four 3D shapes.

Pentagonal prism   Square-based pyramid   Cube   Triangular prism

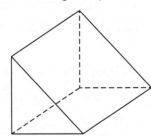

Complete the table to show how many vertices, edges and faces each shape has.

	Pentagonal prism	Square-based pyramid	Cube	Triangular prism
Vertices				
Edges				
Faces				

3 This shape is a cube. Fill in the missing numbers to complete the sentence.

This cube has ☐ faces and ☐ right angles on each face.

4 This is a tangram. A tangram is a square cut up into seven pieces.

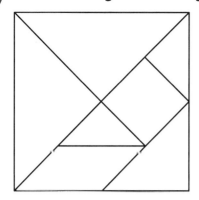

In the tangram:

How many of the pieces are triangles? ▢

How many of the pieces are squares? ▢

How many of the pieces are parallelograms? ▢

How many of the pieces are pentagons? ▢

Evie uses the shapes in the tangram to make two other shapes.
How many lines of symmetry does each shape have?

Evie uses the tangram to make half a shape. The bold line is the mirror line.

Complete the shape.

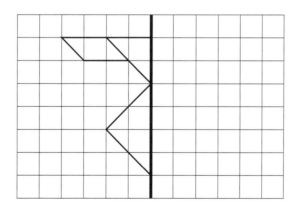

How did you do?   **Questions 1–4**

Circle the star to show how you have done.   Some   Most    All

25

Back at the zoo

1 This is the plan of the zoo. The bold line is a path around the zoo and the black circles are viewing places for each animal.

Parent tip
Remember that when describing a movement, the horizontal movement is written before the vertical movement.

Amir arrives at the zoo entrance (in the top left corner).
Complete the description of the shortest route Amir can take to see the tiger.

[ ] squares down, 1 square _____ , [ ] squares down.

Next, Amir goes on to see the penguin. Complete the description of that route.

[ ] square(s) _____ , 1 square _____ , [ ] squares _____ .

Write a description to show the shortest route from the penguin to the snake.

_____

Write a description to show the shortest route from the snake to the zebra.

_____

Amir has missed out the giraffe and the panda. He chooses the one that is furthest from the zebra. Write a description to show the route from the zebra.

_____

Amir visits the elephant and then walks to the rhino. Write a description to show the shortest route from the elephant to the rhino.

_____

2 This coordinate grid shows the position of animals in another part of the zoo.

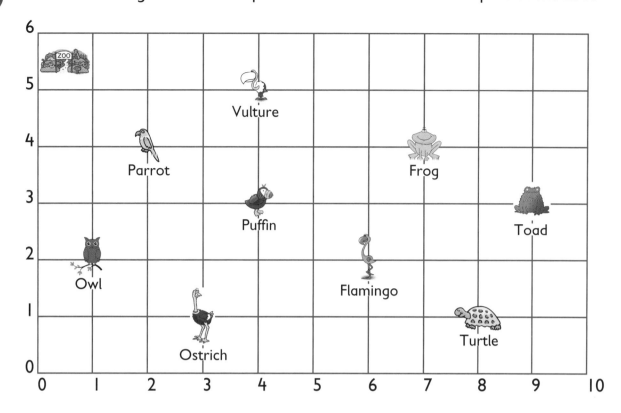

Which animal is at coordinates (7, 4)? _____

Which animal is at coordinates (6, 2)? _____

Which animal is at coordinates (4, 3)? _____

Which animal is at coordinates (9, 3)? _____

What are the coordinates of the vulture? [   ]

What are the coordinates of the owl? [   ]

The manager plans to link coordinates (2, 2), (4, 1), (7, 2) and (9, 1) to make a path. They will form a special type of quadrilateral. Name the type of quadrilateral.

_____

How did you do?

Circle the star to show how you have done.

 Some

 Most

All

Questions 1–2

After-school club

This pictogram shows how many children attend each of the after-school clubs at a school.

After-school clubs	🚶 stands for 2 children
Gym club	🚶🚶🚶🚶🚶🚶🚶🚶🚶🚶🚶🚶🚶🚶🚶🚶🚶🚶🚶╿
Drama club	🚶🚶🚶🚶🚶🚶🚶
Chess club	🚶🚶🚶🚶🚶╿
Football club	🚶🚶🚶🚶🚶🚶🚶🚶🚶🚶
Art club	🚶🚶🚶🚶🚶🚶🚶
Craft club	🚶🚶🚶🚶🚶🚶🚶🚶🚶🚶🚶🚶

1 How many children attend Drama club?

How many children attend Chess club?

Which club is attended by exactly 20 children? _____

How many clubs are attended by fewer than 20 children?

2 How many more children attend Craft club than Art club?

How many fewer children attend Drama club than Gym club?

The school is starting a new club called Puzzle club. There are 18 children interested.

How many child symbols will need to be added to the pictogram for Puzzle club?

How did you do?   Questions 1–2

Circle the star to show how you have done.

Some

Most

All

School dinners

This bar chart shows what type of dinner some school children have.

School dinners

Type of dinner (y-axis), Number of children (x-axis)

- Home dinner: 10
- Packed lunch: 38
- Sandwiches: 44
- Vegetarian: 32
- Cold meal: 40
- Hot meal: 65

x-axis: 0, 10, 20, 30, 40, 50, 60, 70

1 How many children went home for dinner? ☐

How many children are represented by each faint line on the bar chart? ☐

How many children had a vegetarian meal? ☐

Which type of meal was provided for exactly 40 children? _____

2 How many more children had a hot meal than a vegetarian meal? ☐

Hot, cold and vegetarian meals and sandwiches are provided by the school kitchen.

How many meals did the school kitchen provide in total? ☐.

> **Parent tip**
> Ask your child to make up their own questions about the bar chart.

How did you do?   Questions 1–2

Circle the star to show how you have done.

Some

Most

All

On the train

1 This table gives information about four different trains leaving the station near Ash's home. Complete the table.

Train time	08:10	09:30	10:50	12:10	Total
1st Class Adult tickets	46	32	35	37	
2nd Class Adult tickets	207			215	789
1st Class Child tickets	4	2			13
2nd Class Child tickets	18	24	28	34	104
Total	275		256	289	1,056

Parent tip
Start by finding the missing values where there is only **one** unknown value in a column or row.

2 This line graph shows the speed of the 08.00 train at 15-minute intervals.

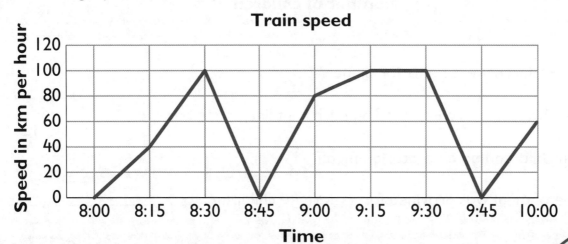

Train speed

What was the speed of the train at 08:15? ☐ km.p.h

According to the graph, how many times did the train

stop on its journey? _____

Explain how you know.

_____

Parent tip
Discuss what you know about the speed of the train in between the time intervals of 15 minutes.

How did you do?   Questions 1-2

Circle the star to show how you have done.

 Some

 Most

 All

30

Answers

At the zoo

1. 24, 28, 32, 36, 40; 8, 16, 24, 32, 40; 42 (sacks)
2. (0)250, (0)300, (0)350, (0)400, (0)450
3. Monday < Tuesday, Wednesday < Sunday, Tuesday = Friday, Thursday > Saturday
4. January < February, June > April, May > April, May > March
5. Tigers, Lions, Giraffes, Chimps, Elephants
6.

Jan	Feb	March	April	May	June
2,854	3,476	6,921	6,096	6,934	6,261

Secret numbers

1. 23 — is three ones less than 40.
   74 — is a number with two tens.
   49 — is three tens more than 40.
   92 — is a number with four tens.
   37 — is a number with two ones.
2. 15; 79; 49
3. 39 only has 3 tens, while 41 has 4 tens
4. A = 10; B = 40; C = Accept an answer of 57–59; D = Accept an answer of 76–78
5. Samir 39; Mandy 57
6. A 55; B 48; C 25
   Ben – Any three of 19, 28, 37, 46, 64, 73, 82, 91
   Max – Any three of 4, 13, 22, 31, 40

At the market

1.

Size	S	M	L	XL
+ 100	336	297	415	206

2.

Size	10	12	14	16	18	20
− 10	205	146	197	114	128	98

3. 500 (total); 406 (left)
4. 111 (jackets)
5. 602 (pairs); 602 − 269 (= 333) **OR** 602 − 333 (= 269)
6. Jan 4,760; Feb 3,900; Mar 5,138; Apr 1,015; May 980; Jun 1,005

Sports day

1. Year 3 = 16, 12, 8; Year 4 = 12, 9, 6; Year 5 = 20, 15, 10; Year 6 = 4 (teams) because 56 ÷ 3 and 56 ÷ 6 do not give whole number answers / have remainders.
2. 64 (hoops); 32 (bean bags); 16 (ropes); 8 (potatoes)
3. 48 (tennis balls); 30 (footballs); 24 (rugby balls); 24 (children); 1,225 (metres) **OR** 1.225 (kilometres)
4. Individual races: 1st place = 72; 2nd place = 32; 3rd place = 18; Total = 122; Team races: 1st place = 72; 2nd place = 24; 3rd place = 12; Total = 108 Total points = 230

At the rugby match

1. North = 4,950; East = 4,080; South = 4,950; West = 4,365 Total = 18,345
2. 810 (fans arrive by coach) 1,310 (fans arrive by car) 2,245 (empty seats). (Accept a correct follow-through from an incorrect total for the West Stand in Q1.)
3. North – 1,694; East – 1,316; South – 1,087. (Accept correct follow-throughs from incorrect totals for any stands in Q1.)
4. North = 105 (programmes); East = 140 (programmes); South = 120 (programmes); West = 168 (programmes) 390 (programmes); 255 (programmes)

Cake and pizza

1. $\frac{9}{10}$; $\frac{1}{10}$; 3 (strawberries); 2 (raspberries)
2. $\frac{1}{6}$ **OR** $\frac{2}{12}$; $\frac{1}{4}$ **OR** $\frac{3}{12}$; 6 is half of 12
3. $\frac{1}{100}$

   $\frac{1}{3} = \frac{2}{6} = \frac{4}{12} = \frac{8}{24} = \frac{12}{36}$
4. Lemon cake $\frac{1}{4}$ (sold) $\frac{3}{4}$ (for sale)

   Walnut cake $\frac{2}{5}$ (sold) $\frac{3}{5}$ (for sale)

   Berry cake $\frac{2}{6}$ **OR** $\frac{1}{3}$ (sold)

   $\frac{4}{6}$ **OR** $\frac{2}{3}$ (for sale)

   Banoffee pie $\frac{1}{8}$ (sold) $\frac{7}{8}$ (for sale)
5. Ben, Josh, Obe, Dev

At the fruit and vegetable stall

1. pears, bananas, plums, strawberries, apples
2. 2 kg; 4 kg; 6 kg; 5 kg
   £1.50; £3; £4.50; £3.75
   The customer is being charged for
   4 kg but only getting 3.6 kg.
3. 0.75 kg (potatoes); 0.25 kg (parsnips);
   0.5 kg (onions); 0.9 kg (sprouts);
   0.3 kg (carrots)
4. £4.23
5. 0.3 kg = 300 g; 0.5 kg = 500 g
6. apples 0.19 kg (Accept 190 g); pears 0.23 kg
   (Accept 230 g); oranges 0.34 kg (Accept 340 g);
   grapefruit 0.63 kg (Accept 630 g);
   melon 1.18 kg (Accept 1,180 g)
7. potatoes £1; flour £3; beans £1.75

Pocket money

1. 5p = **1**, 10p = **2**, 50p = **3**, £1 = **4**, £5 = **5**,
   £10 = **6**
2. £3.15
3. £2.70; £17.55; £6.40; £12.80
4. 20p; 10p + 10p; 10p + 5p + 5p; 5p + 5p +
   5p + 5p
5. £0.65 **OR** 65p; 5 (coins)
   Accept any 6 coins that total 83p, e.g. 20p +
   20p + 20p + 20p + 2p + 1p
6. 4 (child tickets)

A day at school

1. Reading; PE; PE; Morning break;
   half an hour **OR** 30 minutes; English
2. Maths; Assembly; Art; Twenty past one
3. Reading, PE, Maths, English, Art
4. 10 (minutes); 5 (minutes); 1 hour 55 minutes
5. 08:50; 14:10; 15:15; 17:10
6. 65 (days)

At the park

1. 18 m; 32 m; 34 m
2. Play area 1: 34 m, 51 m²;
   Play area 2: 36 m, 57 m²
3. Café: 72 m, 129 m²; Toilets: 18 m, 18 m²;
   Kitchen: 40 m, 51 m²
4. Office: 40 m, 100 m²; Greenhouse: 100 m,
   400 m²; Stores: 46 m, 120 m²

Shapes

1.

Letter	L	H	V	F	T	N
Perpendicular	✓	✓		✓	✓	
Parallel		✓		✓		✓

2.

	Pentagonal prism	Square-based pyramid	Cube	Triangular prism
Vertices	10	5	8	6
Edges	15	8	12	9
Faces	7	5	6	5

3. **6** faces and **4** right angles on each face.
4. 5 (triangles); 1 (square); 1 (parallelogram)
   (Also accept 2 parallelograms if including the
   square); 0 (pentagons)
   1 (line of symmetry); 2 (lines of symmetry)

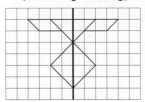

Back at the zoo

1. 2 squares down, 1 square **right, 3** squares down.
   1 square **right,** 1 square **up, 2** squares **right.**
   2 squares right, 1 square down.
   3 squares up, 2 squares right, 2 squares up.
   4 squares left, 1 square down, 3 squares left,
   1 square up.
   1 square up, 1 square left, 2 squares up,
   3 squares left.
2. frog; flamingo; puffin; toad
   (4, 5); (1, 2); parallelogram

After-school club

1. 14 (children); 11 (children);
   Football club; 3 (clubs)
2. 8 (children); 7 (children); 9 (symbols)

School dinners

1. 10 (children); 2 (children); 32 (children); Cold meal
2. 33 (children); 181 (meals)

On the train

1.

Time	08:10	09:30	10:50	12:10	Total
1st, Adult	46	32	35	37	**150**
2nd, Adult	207	**178**	**189**	215	789
1st, Child	4	2	**4**	**3**	13
2nd, Child	18	24	28	34	104
Total	275	**236**	256	289	1,056

2. 40 km.p.h.
   Twice (Accept 08:45 and 09:45) The speed at
   these times is 0 km.p.h.